AGE OF DINOSAURS: **TYRANNOSAURUS REX**

AGE OF DINOSAURS:

Tyrannosaurus Rex

SARA GILBERT

CREATIVE EDUCATION

Published by Creative Education
P.O. Box 227, Mankato, Minnesota 56002
Creative Education is an imprint of The Creative Company
www.thecreativecompany.us

Design and production by Blue Design
Art direction by Rita Marshall
Printed by Corporate Graphics in the United States of America

Photographs by Alamy (EckPhoto, Interfoto, The Print
Collector), Bridgeman Art Library (Francis Phillipps), Corbis
(Bettmann, Close Murray/Corbis Sygma, Louie Psihoyos), Getty
Images (DEA Picture Library, Stephen Wilkes), iStockphoto
(Linda Bucklin, Jeff Chiasson, David Coder, Christoph Ermel,
Micha Fleuren, Anton Foltin, Richard Goerg, Gilles Glod, Klaus
Nilkens, Allan Tooley), Library of Congress, Sarah Yakawonis/
Blue Design

Library of Congress Cataloging-in-Publication Data
Gilbert, Sara.
Tyrannosaurus rex / by Sara Gilbert.
p. cm. — (Age of dinosaurs)
Summary: An introduction to the life and era of the fearsome,
carnivorous dinosaur known as *Tyrannosaurus rex*, starting
with the creature's 1902 discovery and ending with present-
day research topics.
Includes bibliographical references and index.
ISBN 978-1-58341-978-6
1. Tyrannosaurus rex—Juvenile literature. I. Title. II. Series.

QE862.S3.G54 2010
567.912'9—dc22   2009025539

CPSIA: 120109 P01089

First Edition
9 8 7 6 5 4 3 2 1

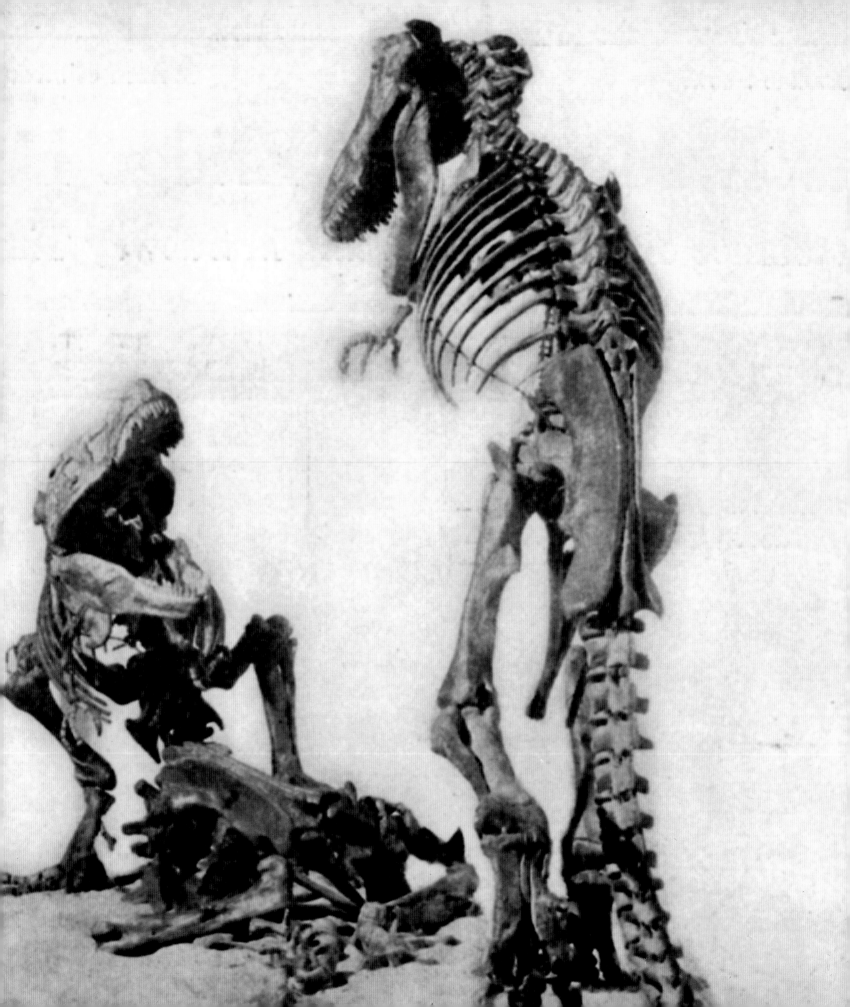

CONTENTS

Dynamite and Digging......................9

King of the Dinosaurs...................17

The End of an Era.......................27

Taming a Tyrant........................37

Glossary...............................47

Selected Bibliography..................47

Read More..............................48

Index..................................48

TYRANNOSAURUS REX TALES

BARNUM "MR. BONES" BROWN 11

HOLES IN THE HEAD 16

CLUES FROM COPROLITE 20

A WORTHY OPPONENT 23

LITTLE TYRANTS 25

MADE FOR THE MOVIES 35

THE SITE FOR SUE 40

BONES AND BOMBS 44

The imposing figure
cut by the killer
Tyrannosaurus rex
is one of the most
recognizable and most
frequently depicted
of all documented
dinosaurs.

DYNAMITE AND DIGGING

Barnum Brown knew that the ragged ravines carved by the Missouri River into the eastern Montana landscape would yield fabulous fossils. Residents had already been finding bones and other remarkable remnants of the past in the area for several years, which was one of the reasons why the skilled fossil hunter had planned a trip there in the summer of 1902.

Brown had yet to celebrate his 30th birthday when he set off for Montana that summer. But he had already been hired on to the staff of the American Museum of Natural History in New York City. Brown had traveled around the world looking for fossils, and he had found so many incredible specimens that some newspapers called him "Mr. Bones." Now the director of the museum, renowned **paleontologist** Henry Fairfield Osborn, had encouraged Brown to take a trip to eastern Montana and explore the exposed Cretaceous **sediment** in the rugged hillsides. Brown was excited for what he might find.

Just weeks after starting to explore the Hell Creek area, Brown and his fellow excavators celebrated their findings of remarkable *Triceratops* fossils. But then, in August, Brown made another discovery that was even more impressive. Embedded in the layers of blue sandstone were enormous bones unlike anything he or any paleontologist had ever seen before. Brown quickly wrote a letter to Osborn, telling him that he had found the remains of a gigantic **carnivorous** dinosaur so solidly secured in sediment that he would have to use dynamite to remove the bones. The pieces were lodged in such a steep slope that horses couldn't be used to pull them out, and there were no jackhammers or other modern machines to help, either. The excavation, Brown predicted, would be lengthy and labor-intensive.

As they set to work in the hot summer sun, Brown and his crew of diggers didn't yet know that the fossilized bones they were unearthing would soon become the most popular dinosaur **species** in the world. However, Brown did realize that he had discovered something of great scientific significance. So he spent the rest of the summer digging out as many bones as he could.

Those bones had to be loaded onto wagons and hauled to the nearest railroad station in Miles City, more than 100 miles (161 km) away from the quarry site at which the men were digging. Once the bones arrived at the station, they were carefully crated and sent to New York on train cars—which cost the museum thousands of dollars. Afterwards, reconstructing the incomplete skeleton took almost three years, as only about half of the specimen's bones had been found. But the expense and time were worth it when, in 1905, Osborn bestowed a suitably ferocious name upon the remains Brown had found: he called the creature *Tyrannosaurus rex*, which means "tyrant lizard king."

As soon as Osborn had officially described the gigantic dinosaur, the public became fascinated with the seemingly terrifying **reptile**. On December 30,

Barnum "Mr. Bones" Brown

Barnum Brown's older brothers and sisters persuaded their parents to name their little brother after the famous circus showman, P. T. Barnum. Little did they know that he would live up to the name, becoming a celebrity in his own right. Brown was considered by many in the scientific world to be the greatest fossil collector of all time. Even though his job was anything but clean-cut, he was always impeccably dressed. He often wore a tie and overcoat while working in the field; once, when he was digging at a quarry in Canada, Brown even opted for a full-length fur coat. Although his dapper dressing was often well documented, his fossil finds generated the most press. In addition to unearthing the first *Tyrannosaurus rex*, he also found a partial *Diplodocus* skeleton and several *Albertosaurus* specimens, among dozens of others. Brown spent most of his adult life working for the American Museum of Natural History, amassing so many boxes of bones that, for long after his death in 1963, some of his well-labeled crates still sat unopened on storeroom shelves in New York.

Paleontologist

Barnum Brown

1905, *The New York Times* ran an article that called *Tyrannosaurus* "the most formidable fighting animal of which there is any record whatever," the "king of all kings in the domain of animal life," "the absolute warlord of the earth," and a "royal man-eater of the jungle."

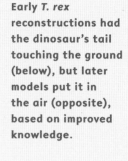

Early *T. rex* reconstructions had the dinosaur's tail touching the ground (below), but later models put it in the air (opposite), based on improved knowledge.

Although many of those descriptions were greatly exaggerated, they were based on what Osborn had been able to learn from the fossilized bones. It was obvious even from those partial remains of *Tyrannosaurus rex*, also known simply as *T. rex*, that it had been one of the most fearsome predators on Earth about 68 million years ago, during the Late Cretaceous Period. It was recognized as a "bipedal theropod," part of a class of meat-eating, predatory dinosaurs that moved on two legs. Its huge head and long, razor-sharp teeth provided definite clues as to how the animal had attacked its prey.

Scientists still had to make many educated guesses about the giant dinosaur's appearance, though. Because not all of the bones of the tail had been located, for instance, they could only theorize that the beast had measured between 40 and 50 feet (12–15 m) in length. Its arms were also a mystery, as only one bone from its upper arm had been found; Osborn's first theory was that the creature's forearms

must have been quite long, in keeping with the proportions of the rest of its body.

Osborn was able to learn more as Brown continued searching for fossils in Hell Creek. By 1908, Brown had dug up the remains of three other *Tyrannosaurus* specimens; he would find two more during his long and illustrious career. The new skeletons Brown brought back to New York were more complete and allowed Osborn to have a

skeletal restoration (made from a combination of specimens) mounted and displayed at the American Museum by 1915.

That display was erected in the pose Osborn believed *T. rex* would have assumed. The bones were arranged in an upright position, with the tail dangling on the ground, in the same way that a modern kangaroo stands. It made an impressive and frightening impression on museum visitors, who popularized the dinosaur and made *T. rex* the most well-known dinosaur species in the world—a status that the great beast never lost, no matter how many other, larger dinosaurs were discovered.

TYRANNOSAURUS REX

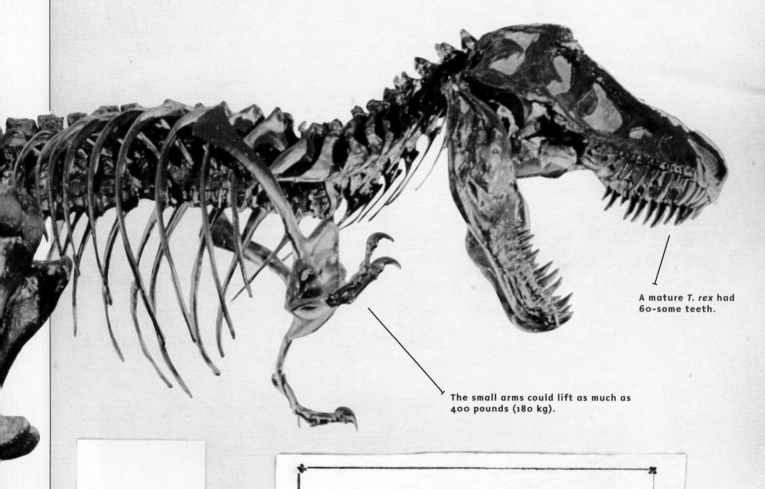

A mature *T. rex* had 60-some teeth.

The small arms could lift as much as 400 pounds (180 kg).

King of the Dinosaurs

T. rex

T. REX SKELETONS were few and far between prior to 1980; only four had been found by then, and those were incomplete. In the past 30 years, about 24 skeletons have been unearthed, giving scientists a clearer picture of the dinosaur's anatomy, or bodily structure.

N. 7705

Holes in the Head

Tyrannosaurus rex had a huge head. It was long and heavy and extremely powerful. But such a heavy head must have been hard to carry around. It is certainly tricky for museums to mount. At 600 pounds (272 kg), the skull of "Sue," the famous *T. rex* displayed at The Field Museum in Chicago, Illinois, is too heavy to be mounted with the rest of its skeleton; it had to be placed on a reinforced stand of its own, while a much lighter cast was put on the skeleton. In real life, a *T. rex*'s skull could have been even heavier if not for the gaps that were built into the bones near the top of the head. Some scientists believe that those holes might have helped absorb the impact when a *Tyrannosaurus* crashed into its prey by allowing room for both the bones and the brain to shift. There might also have been flexible connections, like ligaments, filling those gaps, making the bones less susceptible to injury. Such theories help explain why a number of remarkably intact fossilized skulls have been recovered by fossil hunters.

KING OF THE DINOSAURS

The early image of *Tyrannosaurus rex* as a dominant, vicious predator has been largely confirmed by scientific study over the past century. In the years since Barnum Brown found the first specimen, approximately 30 skeletons have been unearthed, including recent finds that are much more complete. Those discoveries have helped paleontologists paint an even more terrifying picture of the "tyrant lizard king."

Tyrannosaurus could easily have measured 45 feet (14 m) from the top of its huge head to the end of its stiff, pointed tail. It stood an imposing 15 to 20 feet (4.5–6 m) tall; its back legs were as tall as two adult men, and on each leg were three birdlike toes equipped with long, sharp claws. In contrast to Osborn's original idea, however, its two front arms were tiny—only about as long as a human's arm—and had just two fingers on each. How *Tyrannosaurus* used its arms, if at all, has long been a source of speculation for scientists.

Those arms were the only things that were small about *Tyrannosaurus*, though. Its skull alone may have been up to 5 feet (1.5 m) long and probably weighed 600 pounds (272 kg) or more. Although the heft of its head added to its power, it was what was inside the skull that struck fear into most other dinosaurs of the Cretaceous Period. Two baseball-sized eyeballs were set up high and faced forward, enabling the dinosaur to see clearly at great distances.

Its large nostrils gave it a keen sense of smell, and its brain, though narrow, was one of the largest among known dinosaur species.

The most intimidating part of *T. rex*, however, was its enormous jaws, which could open wide enough to swallow an adult human being in one bite. Inside those jaws were more than 50 jagged teeth, which were replaced quickly when one broke or fell out. Each of those sharp teeth was between 6 and 12 inches (15–30 cm) long and curved backwards. When *Tyrannosaurus* found something to bite into, it could easily pull off enormous chunks of flesh.

To maintain a constant body weight, the five-ton (4.5 t) carnivore needed to ingest incredible amounts of meat daily. Some scientists suspect that a typical *Tyrannosaurus* would have needed to eat its weight in meat on a weekly basis. That means that it would have been perpetually on the lookout for a new source of food. *Tyrannosaurus* was not picky. It is known to have eaten many of the **herbivorous** dinosaurs that shared the planet during the Cretaceous Period. Even the four-ton (3.6 t) *Edmontosaurus* and the armored *Triceratops* fell prey to the terrible *Tyrannosaurus*, as is evidenced by those species' fossilized bones, which show the telltale deep gashes of *T. rex* teeth. The fossilized droppings, or coprolites, of

It is likely that the only way *T. rex* could prey upon a heavily armored dinosaur such as *Euoplocephalus* was to flip it over, exposing its soft underbelly.

Coprolite

Clues from Coprolite

There are many ways scientists can learn about the life of *Tyrannosaurus rex*. They can study its bones, look at its fossilized footprints, and even analyze the rocks in which it was buried. They can also look for clues in its fossilized droppings, which are known as coprolites. Coprolites are hard to find, due to their indistinct shape and the ease with which they can be broken apart or washed away. But they can reveal important information about what dinosaurs ate. So when a team of scientists in the Canadian province of Saskatchewan found an enormous 17-inch (43 cm) coprolite near a bed of *Tyrannosaurus* bones, they eagerly took it back to the lab with them and cut it into paper-thin slices. When they looked at the slices under a microscope, they could see tiny pieces of bones that had been partially digested by the dinosaur. By analyzing the patterns of the blood vessels in those fragments, they could decipher that the bones had likely come from a young plant-eating dinosaur, meaning that the coprolite had been produced by a carnivore and probably a *Tyrannosaurus rex* at that.

Tyrannosaurus have also revealed bone fragments belonging to plant-eaters such as *Triceratops*.

Exactly how *Tyrannosaurus* obtained its food is not clear. Its tall, muscular legs allowed it to move quickly, taking strides that were 12 to 15 feet (4–5 m) long and possibly reaching speeds between 10 and 20 miles (16–32 km) per hour. Such speeds would have enabled it to chase down heavier and slower dinosaurs, but some scientists believe that it would have been difficult for *Tyrannosaurus* to chase its prey at such speeds for very far. Although it is now clear that it would have used its tail for balance while running, instead of dragging it behind as Osborn originally thought, its small, useless arms would not have been able to help break its fall if it stumbled in its forested habitat.

Another theory is that *Tyrannosaurus* was a crafty hunter that lurked among plant life such as evergreens and early oak trees before lunging out at its prey. It likely waited to attack until prey such as a

When *T. rex* lost or broke a tooth, a new one would grow in its place, so adult specimens are often found having teeth of varying sizes.

young duck-billed dinosaur wandered away from its herd or a weak or sick animal presented itself. It's also possible that *Tyrannosaurus* traveled in teams, ganging up on such well-armed opponents as *Triceratops* to make a kill together.

Other scientists think that *Tyrannosaurus* didn't actually hunt at all. They speculate that the lumbering beast couldn't maintain fast enough speeds to cover much ground and therefore would not have been able to catch more nimble prey. Instead, they think that *T. rex* was a scavenger that followed behind the **migratory** herds of herbivores and picked the flesh off of dead or dying dinosaurs when they fell.

Triceratops **and its horned relatives were tough prey for** *T. rex*, **but** *Triceratops*'**s natural defenses did not stop the carnivore from trying.**

The truth may lie somewhere in between the hunting and scavenging theories. It is unlikely that such a large animal could have survived simply on the meat found on rotting corpses; no large, land-based meat-eater living today is able to survive on such carrion alone. But if a *Tyrannosaurus* came upon a dead animal, it is also unlikely that it would have passed up the opportunity to eat. *Tyrannosaurus*, like other meat-eating theropods such as *Allosaurus* and *Albertosaurus*, was probably both a hunter and a scavenger. Although evidence suggests that *Tyrannosaurus* lived in familial groups, hunting and raising their young together, it is also possible that they may have

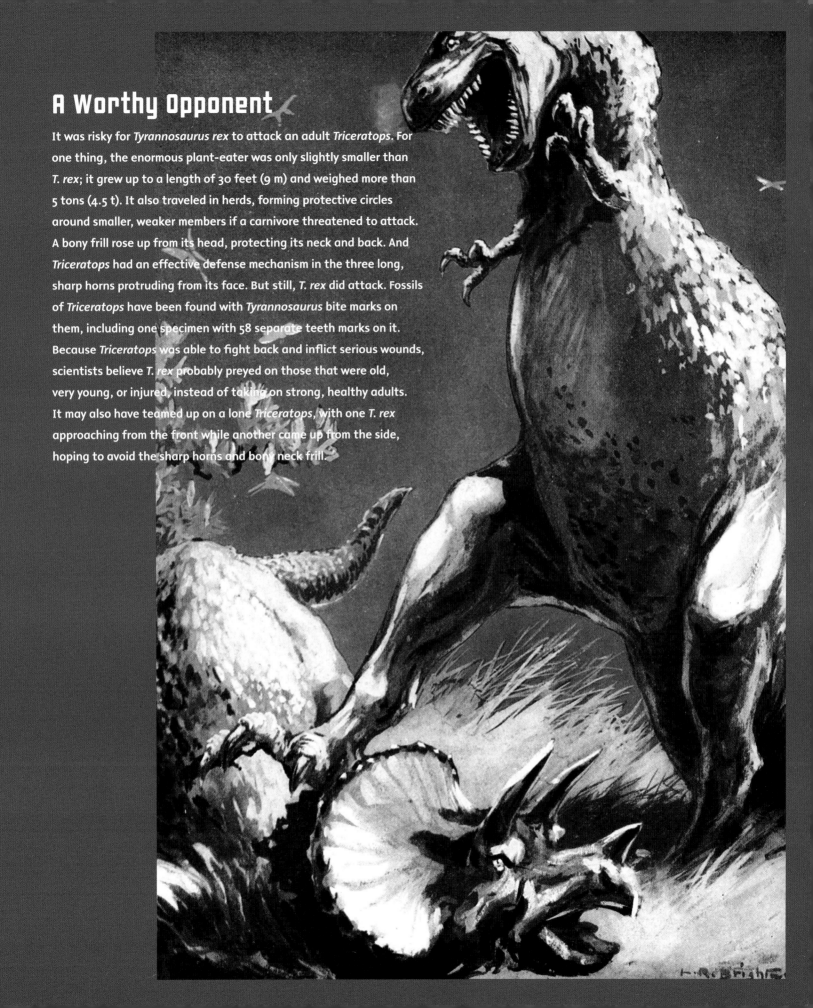

A Worthy Opponent

It was risky for *Tyrannosaurus rex* to attack an adult *Triceratops*. For one thing, the enormous plant-eater was only slightly smaller than *T. rex*; it grew up to a length of 30 feet (9 m) and weighed more than 5 tons (4.5 t). It also traveled in herds, forming protective circles around smaller, weaker members if a carnivore threatened to attack. A bony frill rose up from its head, protecting its neck and back. And *Triceratops* had an effective defense mechanism in the three long, sharp horns protruding from its face. But still, *T. rex* did attack. Fossils of *Triceratops* have been found with *Tyrannosaurus* bite marks on them, including one specimen with 58 separate teeth marks on it. Because *Triceratops* was able to fight back and inflict serious wounds, scientists believe *T. rex* probably preyed on those that were old, very young, or injured, instead of taking on strong, healthy adults. It may also have teamed up on a lone *Triceratops*, with one *T. rex* approaching from the front while another came up from the side, hoping to avoid the sharp horns and bony neck frill.

fought amongst themselves. *Tyrannosaurus* skeletons have been found with the teeth of other *Tyrannosaurus* lodged within their **vertebrae**. Because the fierce predator was at the top of the **food chain**, it likely had no natural enemies other than itself.

Fossil finds suggest that *T. rex* was rarely preyed upon, even when young. Very few juvenile *Tyrannosaurus* skeletons have been found, which indicates that the dinosaur often survived into adulthood. The most mature *T. rex* specimen scientists have been able to date was likely 28 years old, and some scientists speculate that it may have been able to live for 30 or 40 years. Although that is still much shorter than the possible 100-year lifespan of the enormous, long-necked **sauropods** that lived during the earlier Jurassic Period, *T. rex* likely outlived many of its smaller contemporaries. As long as there were plenty of meaty plant-eaters around for *T. rex* to consume, it was able to flourish for a long time.

Using a technique similar to counting tree rings, scientists are able to gauge a dinosaur's age from its bones and determine *T. rex*'s growth rate.

Little Tyrants

Until 1998, very little was known about the early years of a *Tyrannosaurus*'s life. But then an amateur fossil hunter named Ron Frithiof discovered the remains of a young *T. rex* in a South Dakota field and named it "Tinker," after his own childhood nickname. Three years later, another juvenile specimen named "Jane" was unearthed in Montana. Since then, Tinker and Jane have opened a window on the childhood of North America's largest carnivore. Paleontologists hope that studying the young dinosaurs' bones will help them understand the growth patterns of the species. The little tyrant kings had an awkward, gangly start: their feet seem to have been overly large in proportion to their bodies, while their shins and ankles were unusually long. Tinker was probably 23 feet (7 m) long, while Jane was a couple of feet shorter. They may have weighed between 1,200 and 1,500 pounds (544–680 kg)—about a quarter of a full-grown *Tyrannosaurus*'s weight. But given that the young specimens were equipped with jaws and teeth that one paleontologist described as "100 percent adult," it's likely that they were able to grow quickly.

Tyrannosaurs first
appeared during the
Late Jurassic Period,
but it took almost 100
million years for them
to achieve their full
potential in *T. rex*.

THE END OF AN ERA

*T*yrannosaurus rex was not around when the Cretaceous Period began about 144 million years ago. By the time *T. rex* entered the scene toward the end of the Cretaceous, between 68 and 65 million years ago, the earth was beginning to take on more of its modern form.

The supercontinent of Pangaea, which included almost all of Earth's landmasses, had already broken up, and the two major fragments that remained—Laurasia in the north and Gondwana in the south—had begun to separate between approximately 180 and 200 million years ago. The seven continents on Earth today eventually broke away and slowly drifted toward their current locations. As they moved, the continents collided with pieces of the ocean floor, causing the formation of several mountain ranges around the world— including the Rocky Mountains in what is now western North America.

All that shifting of landmasses also caused sea levels to rise and **climates** to change in different parts of the world. Although the world had grown warmer and wetter during the period prior to the Cretaceous, the Jurassic, now temperatures climbed even higher. Such warm temperatures resulted in the creation of subtropical landscapes as far north as where the state of New York is located today.

That warmer weather allowed more plant

The skulls of tyrannosaurs were massive, and the longest specimen on record measures more than four feet (1.2 m).

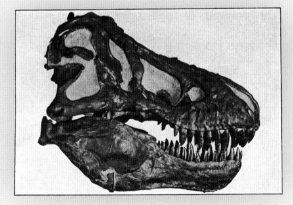

life to flourish. Small flowering plants began coloring a landscape otherwise dominated by the browns and greens of **cycads**, **conifers**, **ginkgoes**, and ferns. By the time *Tyrannosaurus* appeared, the first broadleaf trees—including oaks, maples, and walnuts—were also sprouting up.

The diversification of vegetation encouraged the **evolution** of more dinosaurs as well. Research indicates that, very late in the Cretaceous Period, the number of dinosaur species on Earth increased substantially—perhaps by as much as 50 percent. Some scientists contend that this may be an inaccurate count, since Late Cretaceous fossils are located closer to the earth's surface and may be easier to find than those from earlier periods. This would make it appear as though there were more species in existence. Other scientists, however, believe that the conditions favored explosive growth, especially among herbivores, as they developed the sharper teeth necessary to tear through the new plant life that was becoming prominent.

Although the giant sauropods of North America, including *Apatosaurus* and *Diplodocus*, had died out by the beginning of the Cretaceous Period, a new group of plant-eaters was evolving. The ornithischian, or bird-hipped, dinosaurs were built to enjoy the new flowering plants in abundance. Duck-bills such as *Edmontosaurus* foraged for food in herds that numbered in the thousands. Horned dinosaurs such as *Triceratops* and *Torosaurus*, as well as the heavily

The meat-eating *T. rex* dominated its Late Cretaceous landscape (opposite) during a time when the continents were becoming more distinct.

armored *Ankylosaurus*, grew numerous. As the Cretaceous Period marched on, the time was right for a great predator to come into the picture. Although *Tyrannosaurus* had direct competition from other carnivores that lived at the same time, including the much smaller *Troodon*, none was as fierce or as feared.

It wasn't just other dinosaurs that feared *Tyrannosaurus*, though. Although dinosaurs were by far the most dominant animals on land, other reptiles and **mammals** were evolving and diversifying rapidly. The first snakes had appeared, as had early crocodiles, and mice, rats, and ancestors of modern opossums scampered through the underbrush. Flying reptiles called pterosaurs ruled the skies, but small birds were becoming more common and were developing their modern skeletal structures and feathers. The advent of flowering plants such as magnolias also brought about the first bees and other flying insects.

Some scientists believe that although *Tyrannosaurus* was clearly a land animal, it was also a good swimmer, capable of pursuing prey through the water as well as on land. It is unlikely, however, that it ventured too far into the deep Cretaceous seas, where giant marine lizards called mosasaurs were among the most feared predators. Sea turtles were also common, in much the same form as they remain today. They fed on small teleosts, an evolved species of fish with lighter scales than its predecessors—an adaptation that

allowed it to swim faster. Most modern fish are descendants of these early teleosts.

Tyrannosaurus may well have been king of the North American dinosaurs, but recent discoveries call into question the idea that the giant reptile was the largest carnivore of its time. The massive *Giganotosaurus*, which was 45 feet (14 m) long and weighed 8 tons (7 t), terrorized the herbivores of South America at approximately the same time as *Tyrannosaurus*, but its fossils were not discovered until 1993.

Although both *Tyrannosaurus* and *Giganotosaurus* were at the top of their respective food chains, neither survived the disaster known as the K-T (Cretaceous-Tertiary) **extinction** event that wiped out all of the remaining dinosaurs and many of the other species of life at the end of the Cretaceous Period. Scientists have speculated for decades about what caused this mass extinction, and numerous theories have been discussed.

One possible cause involves the volcanoes that became increasingly active during the Cretaceous Period. Scientists know that at some point around the time of extinction, about 65 million years ago, there was a series of enormous volcanic eruptions on Earth. Clouds of dust and gases would have filled the sky, blocking a significant amount of sunlight and resulting in a prolonged cooling effect. This would have led to a mass extinction of the larger animals unable to withstand such temperatures.

Most scientists, however, believe that *Tyrannosaurus* and the rest of the dinosaurs were destroyed by a major catastrophe caused by an impact from outer space. A meteor measuring approximately six miles (9.7 km) across is known to have struck the planet 65 million years ago near the coast of Mexico's Yucatán Peninsula. The impact likely resulted in a climate-changing scenario similar to the volcanic eruptions. Some scientists have even speculated that the dinosaurs—and other life on Earth—may have fallen victim to a combination of catastrophes around the same time. Although exactly what happened may never be known, the results are undeniable. Only about three million years after *Tyrannosaurus rex* first appeared on Earth, it disappeared.

Made for the Movies

No dinosaur has had as many starring roles as *Tyrannosaurus rex*. It has appeared in dozens of movies and television shows, from such classic films as *King Kong* to children's television favorites such as *Barney and Friends* and *The Wiggles*. Although its depiction is not always realistic (as is the case with the good-natured character of Barney), most serious films try to at least draw from scientific fact. Those facts have sometimes been blurred, however. Early films portrayed *T. rex* with a third finger on its arms, much like *Allosaurus*, a carnivore of the Jurassic Period. Producer Walt Disney reportedly told Barnum Brown that "it looked better that way." By the time *Jurassic Park* was released in 1993, the anatomy had improved—as had the special effects. In the movie, a terrifying *T. rex* is one of several dinosaurs brought back to life at a theme park, where it kills one person and wounds another. More recently, a *T. rex* skeleton at the American Museum of Natural History in New York City had a starring role in the 2006 film *Night at the Museum* and its 2009 sequel.

TAMING A TYRANT

When the first *Tyrannosaurus* bones were discovered in Montana in 1902, the scientists who studied them had to make assumptions based on the information they had access to at the time. Further research proved that some of those assumptions had been correct. But as more fossils have been found and more sophisticated methods of studying them have been developed, a more complete understanding of the "tyrant lizard king" has emerged.

One of the most visible changes relates to the dinosaur's posture. Early skeletal models showed *Tyrannosaurus* in an upright "tripod" pose, its head held high and its tail propping it up from behind. Such a pose, designed to give the creature an imposing and intimidating stance, seemed applicable to a carnivore of its stature. Now, however, scientists know that maintaining such a posture probably wouldn't have been possible. Instead, they believe that *Tyrannosaurus* walked with its back level, its head slightly raised, and its tail held stiffly out behind it, probably to help the weighty beast maintain its balance.

That more accurate picture of how *Tyrannosaurus* held its body has led to changes in how reconstructed skeletons are displayed at museums such as the American and Carnegie Museums of Natural History. Although scientists began to realize what *T. rex*'s true position was in the 1970s, many paintings, films, and museum reconstructions continued using the outdated tripod pose until the

Paleontologists have revised their theories over the years, moving away from the belief that *T. rex* stood upright and dragged its tail behind.

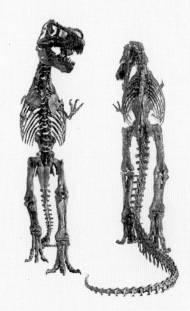

1990s. Reassembling a *Tyrannosaurus* skeleton is a complicated task that requires the expertise of paleontologists as well as **engineers** and **blacksmiths**. Being able to portray a more scientifically accurate model of the dinosaur is costly, but the price is worth it to most institutions.

One of the long-standing questions that has plagued scientists about *Tyrannosaurus* is how it used its front arms. Although the answer remains a mystery, much progress has been made since complete forearm fossils were found by a Montana family in 1988. John Horner, a paleontologist with Montana State University's Museum of the Rockies, studied those bones. He was surprised to find out that although the approximately three-foot-long (0.9 m) arms were not much bigger than a human's, they would have been quite muscular. *T. rex* would have been able to lift the equivalent of two adult men with its arms alone.

The arms were too short to reach *T. rex*'s mouth, so they weren't helpful for feeding. However, scientists reason that because there were two sharp claws at the end of each arm, the claws might have been used to grip prey after it was caught. The arms might also have been useful when the beast needed to push itself up off the ground.

Each new *T. rex* breakthrough offers scientists more insight into the dinosaur's existence. Fossil hunter Sue Hendrickson's 1990 discovery of the almost complete skeleton "Sue" has allowed scientists to learn more about the dinosaur's physical makeup. Sue's bones were so well

The Site for Sue

Visitors to The Field Museum in Chicago pay nothing more than the standard museum admission fee to see "Sue," a 42-foot-long (12.8 m) and 13-foot-tall (4 m) *Tyrannosaurus rex* skeleton that is the most complete *T. rex* specimen displayed anywhere in the world. But in order to obtain Sue's 200-plus bones and put them on display, The Field Museum had to pay a steep price: nearly $8.4 million. A fossil hunter named Sue Hendrickson discovered Sue on August 12, 1990, and almost immediately, controversy arose over who owned the bones. When a judge ruled that the rancher who owned the land on which the bones were found was the rightful owner of the bones, that rancher put the skeleton up for auction. Just eight minutes after the auction opened on October 4, 1997, The Field Museum had placed the winning bid. Museum staff spent more than 25,000 hours preparing Sue for display and even had to call in jewelry makers to help create the steel supports for her bones. On May 17, 2000, almost 10,000 people witnessed the unveiling of the reconstructed skeleton.

preserved in a South Dakota cliff that paleontologists could actually tell where muscles had been attached and where bones had been broken and healed. Not only were they able to create a much clearer picture of what the muscles of the leg looked like, but they were also able to tell how old Sue had been by analyzing a **cross-section** of a leg bone; scientists came to the conclusion that the dinosaur was 28 years old when it died.

Sue also provided an important clue about the relationship between dinosaurs and modern birds. Sue was found with an intact furcula, or wishbone—which birds also have. Many scientists believe that that bone points to an evolutionary link between dinosaurs, especially theropods such as *Tyrannosaurus*, and the birds of today. Both birds and dinosaurs have the same hip sockets, with a distinct hole where the leg bone connects to the rest of the body. Additionally, all of the theropods, including *Tyrannosaurus*, had hollow bones, just like birds. Birds also share a special moon-shaped bone in their wrists with a group of small predatory dinosaurs called maniraptors. Although some scientists remain skeptical that birds and dinosaurs are related, others continue to search for clues that might prove their kinship.

Recently, paleontologists studying other *T. rex* specimens have made important breakthroughs that could lead to a better understanding of how *T. rex* and other dinosaurs are connected to modern birds and mammals. In 2005, a team of scientists was

Studying fossilized bones is often theoretical work, based largely on educated guesses, until enough specimens can be found to confirm those theories.

The first bones from the *T. rex* known as "Stan" were discovered in South Dakota in 1987 by amateur paleontologist Stan Sacrison.

able to isolate fossilized soft tissue—including blood vessels and cells—from inside a 70-million-year-old *Tyrannosaurus* bone. Later, another scientist was able to retrieve proteins in their natural form from a *T. rex* leg bone. Scientists studying those proteins have found that they are more similar to the proteins contained in the bones of chickens and ostriches than they are to those of alligators and other reptiles. This leads some scientists to suspect that the prehistoric reptiles may have been warm-blooded instead of cold-blooded.

Ten years after Sue was unearthed, Horner and a crew of fossil hunters found five more remarkable *T. rex* skeletons buried close together in Montana. Three more were found the following summer, in

Bones and Bombs

There were many reasons for concern when the U.S. entered World War II in 1941. Mothers and wives were worried about the sons and husbands who were fighting against German and Japanese forces abroad. Factory owners were worried about who would fill all of the jobs left empty. Almost everyone was worried about how long the war would last and whether or not its violence would spread to American soil. With that very thought in mind, the directors of New York's American Museum of Natural History became concerned about the fate of the *Tyrannosaurus rex* skeleton that was displayed there. Many fossils in European museums had been blown to bits by bombings in the 1930s, and if the war reached the U.S., no one wanted to lose the prized *T. rex* skeleton Barnum Brown had unearthed in Montana. So that skeleton was shipped to Pittsburgh, where it was placed in the Carnegie Museum of Natural History for safekeeping. The Carnegie Museum ended up buying that skeleton, and it continues to be featured in Pittsburgh today, although the posture has since been modernized.

2001, including one that may be even larger than Sue. Parts of those skeletons are on display at the Museum of the Rockies in Bozeman, Montana, including what may be the largest *T. rex* skull in the world. Many other museums also have *Tyrannosaurus* skeletons as part of their collections. Sue, for example, belongs to The Field Museum in Chicago, and a skeleton recreated from some of Barnum Brown's early finds is still shown at the American Museum of Natural History in New York. Other specimens are also housed at the Royal Tyrrell Museum in Alberta, Canada, the Denver Museum of Natural History in Colorado, and the Academy of Natural Sciences in Philadelphia.

Both professional paleontologists and amateur fossil hunters have been able to add to museum collections, thanks to the numerous technological advances since Barnum Brown used dynamite to remove the first *Tyrannosaurus* bones in 1902. People have also benefited from improvements made in how bones can be studied as well; scientists can now use modern medical equipment, including X-rays, to analyze the bones, and computer simulations allow them to reconstruct the dinosaurs' bodies.

Any time scientists learn something new about *Tyrannosaurus* or another dinosaur, they come closer to understanding what life on Earth was like millions of years ago. More than 100 years after the first *Tyrannosaurus* bones were discovered, scientists are still learning more about them and their reptilian relatives. And a century from now, they will probably have still more to discover.

While individual teeth (above) and other dinosaur parts are relatively common, complete skeletons (opposite) are hard to come by and even more challenging to preserve.

T-Rex compared with a five-foot-tall (152 cm) human

GLOSSARY

blacksmiths—people who make things, including horseshoes and structural beams, out of iron

carnivorous—describing an animal that feeds on other animals

climates—the long-term weather conditions of areas

conifers—evergreen trees, such as pines and firs, that bear cones

cross-section—a piece cut off a whole bone or other item to allow scientists to study the item's center

cycads—tropical palmlike plants that bear large cones

engineers—people who use specific scientific knowledge to solve problems

evolution—the process of adapting or changing over time to survive in a certain environment

extinction—the act or process of becoming extinct; coming to an end or dying out

food chain—a system in nature in which living things are dependent upon each other for food

ginkgoes—large, ornamental trees with fan-shaped leaves, fleshy fruit, and edible nuts

herbivorous—describing an animal that feeds only on plants

mammals—warm-blooded animals that have a backbone and hair or fur, give birth to live young, and produce milk to feed their young

migratory—related to traveling from one region or climate to another for feeding or breeding purposes

paleontologist—a scientist who studies fossilized plants and animals

reptile—a cold-blooded animal with scaly skin that typically lays eggs on land

sauropods—large, four-legged, plant-eating dinosaurs that had long necks and tails

sediment—crushed, rocky matter that settles to the bottom of a liquid, such as a body of water

species—a group of living organisms that share similar characteristics and can mate with one another

vertebrae—the series of small bones forming the backbone

SELECTED BIBLIOGRAPHY

Barrett, Paul. *National Geographic Dinosaurs*. Washington, D.C.: National Geographic Society, 2001.

Burnie, David. *The Kingfisher Illustrated Dinosaur Encyclopedia*. New York: Kingfisher Publications, 2001.

Dingus, Lowell. *Hell Creek Montana*. New York: St. Martin's Press, 2004.

Farlow, James O., and M. K. Brett-Surman. *The Complete Dinosaur*. Bloomington, Ind.: Indiana University Press, 1997.

Fiffer, Steve. *Tyrannosaurus Sue*. New York: W. H. Freeman and Company, 2000.

Lambert, David. *The Ultimate Dinosaur Book*. New York: DK Publishing, 1993.

INDEX

Academy of Natural Sciences 45

American Museum of Natural History 9, 11, 14, 35, 37, 44, 45
  skeletal reconstructions 14, 37, 44, 45

Brown, Barnum 9–10, 11, 14, 17, 35, 44, 45

Carnegie Museum of Natural History 37, 44

competition from other carnivores 30

coprolites 18, 20

Cretaceous Period 13, 17, 18, 21, 25, 27, 29–30, 33–34
  animal life 29, 30, 33
  climate 27
  contemporaries of *T. rex* 18, 25, 29, 33
  landmass shifting 27
  plant life 21, 27, 29, 30

Denver Museum of Natural History 45

extinction 33–34

first *T. rex* bones 9–10, 11, 13, 17, 37, 45

Frithiof, Ron 25

geographical range 25, 29, 33

Horner, John 38, 42

Jurassic Period 25, 27, 35

juvenile specimens 25

life expectancy 25, 41

Museum of the Rockies 38, 45

Osborn, Henry Fairfield 9, 10, 13, 14, 17, 21
  naming of *T. rex* 10

physical characteristics 13–14, 16, 17, 18, 21, 22, 23, 25, 35, 37, 38, 40, 41, 42, 44, 45
  arms 13–14, 17, 35, 38

brain 16, 18

claws 17, 38

growth rate 25

head 13, 16, 17, 45

legs 17, 21, 41, 42

sizes 13, 16, 17, 25, 40

skeletal similarities to birds 41

soft tissue 42

speed 21, 22

stance 14, 37, 44

tail 13, 14, 17, 21, 37

teeth 13, 18, 23, 25

warm-blooded versus cold-blooded theories 42

popular culture references 35

prey 13, 16, 18, 21, 22, 23, 25, 29, 38
  Ankylosaurus 29
  Edmontosaurus 18, 29
  Torosaurus 29
  Triceratops 18, 21, 22, 23, 29

revised assumptions 37–38

Royal Tyrrell Museum 45

"Sue" specimen 16, 38, 40, 41, 42, 45
  at The Field Museum 16, 40, 45
  discovery by Sue Hendrickson 38, 40
  payment for 40

theropods 13, 22, 25, 41
  living in groups 22, 25

READ MORE

Horner, John R., and Don Lessem. *Digging up Tyrannosaurus Rex*. New York: Crown Publishers, 1992.

Lansky, Kathryn. *Dinosaur Dig*. New York: Morrow Junior Books, 1990.

Matthews, Rupert. *Dinosaur Dictionary*. New York: Tangerine Press, 2001.

Schomp, Virginia. *Tyrannosaurus and Other Giant Meat-Eaters*. New York: Marshall Cavendish Children, 2003.